About the Author

A lover of life enthusiast spreading love and light into the world.

I am many things and I wear many hats in my life. To narrow it down, I am a grateful mother to a beautiful daughter. I am ambitious and career driven always striving to be the best that I can be, whilst seeking the next challenge in my life.

From a very young age, I remember, I was always on a mission, on a quest and learning new things was where I felt I would thrive best. I enjoyed reading, and in particular reading poetry. Poetry became a passion of mine from a young age because this is where I felt I could escape, and now, where I can share with the world where my imagination takes me. With that in mind, it is no surprise to me that I am here today at the ending process of publishing my own poetry book.

I was always a curious soul about realms out of this world, and the endless possibilities of why, what and where. I would always ask questions and challenge things I would see, read or hear in many of the daily environments I was surrounded by. I am a truth teller. I seek the truth. My motto in life is to be good, do good or as Ghandi put it. "Be the change you want to see in the world".

I aim to be understanding, helpful and in any way possible to be guiding others, a sentiment that has been instilled in me from a young age. Maybe from the unconditional love my mother gifted me, or lack of, where others did not. I can't answer, but the last few years this powerful urge has awoken in me. An urge I feel is leading me to my purpose, my existence in this world.

I became a mother for the first time, in 2015, and a maternal instinct kicked in. My daughter gave me the strength to take a stand, to speak up for not only her or myself but for anyone who would somehow be faced with similar predicaments in life as me.

So here I am, on this quest and journey of 'awakening', I aim to become the best version of myself that I can in order to serve others in a positive way.

I see strength in all my experiences in life and I am grateful because it is those experiences that made me who I am today. Through my poetry I take you on that journey, a journey of enlightenment.

Words in a Heartbeat

Liri Begaj

Words in a Heartbeat

Olympia Publishers
London

www.olympiapublishers.com
OLYMPIA PAPERBACK EDITION

Copyright © Liri Begaj 2020

The right of Liri Begaj to be identified as author of
this work has been asserted in accordance with sections 77 and 78
of the Copyright, Designs and Patents Act 1988.

All Rights Reserved

No reproduction, copy or transmission of this publication
may be made without written permission.
No paragraph of this publication may be reproduced,
copied or transmitted save with the written permission of the
publisher, or in accordance with the provisions
of the Copyright Act 1956 (as amended).

Any person who commits any unauthorised act in relation to
this publication may be liable to criminal
prosecution and civil claims for damage.

A CIP catalogue record for this title is
available from the British Library.

ISBN: 978-1-78830-548-8

First Published in 2020

Olympia Publishers
Tallis House
2 Tallis Street
London
EC4Y 0AB

Printed in Great Britain

Acknowledgements

Thankful to the experiences that made me.

I dedicate this book to my darling daughter, Amelia.

The Agony of a Broken Heart

Momentarily
You left me, empty
Inside.
You killed a part of me
That night.

My bleeding heart
Pouring
Bloody
Words
Everywhere
My Love.

I dreaded
The thought of
Things no longer
Being the same.
Then the morning came.

I felt the agony of a broken heart
For the first time.
A feeling
You couldn't ever comprehend
Even if you tried.

BUT
As I said
Only momentarily,
It felt like countless seconds
Where my heart
Was chained.
Like a spiral of repeated strikes
Of pain.
But little did you know
I define strength.
So mending a broken heart,
I could bear this pain.

Signed, Freedom
@wordsinaheartbeat

Phoenix

Oh how trivial it all seems.
What felt like endless years
Were only the same moments relived.
Demons no longer chasing me
I've faced those fears
Whilst counting down my river tears.

I have now gained strength to
Chase my dreams
I am a soulful force
Not to be reckoned with.

Oh how trivial it all seems.
For now I understand
All the countless times I cried
You were written in my stars.
As a testament,
In the worst way, a helping hand.

You
Awakened the Phoenix in me.
And finally I can see
My purpose in this life,
My destiny.

Signed, Freedom
@wordsinaheartbeat

God's Plan

Her emotions,
Translated into tears once more.
Justified by the heaviness in her heart.
A burden he had imprinted there
Right from the start.
He left her breathless, drowning in hurt.
But nothing could make her bitter.
No matter how bitter his love was.
She knew this was God's plan.
And although he couldn't understand
She rose up, head held high, with a smile.
She dried her own tears for the last time.

Signed, Freedom
@wordsinaheartbeat

Hopeless Feelings

Imagine feeling your heart breaking
Piece by piece, into pieces.
Like little fragments, of hopeless feelings
Like the reflection of glass from a broken mirror.

You broke my heart, so repeatedly.
You had me, at my weakest.
But it was more so, that,
You knew how genuine my heart was
And yet you still broke it so willingly.

That's what really hurt me the most.

Signed, Freedom
@wordsinaheartbeat

The Moon spoke to Her

She didn't know
How to
Let him go
Or where
To find the strength
To do so.

She'd often look up in hope,
In desperate search for answers
But like the heavens and earth were separated
She felt all alone.
Like souls departed
From their bodies, so unjustly.

The skies dark and she hopeless
As the brightest stars' light dimmed.
But little did she know
The stars dying were fulfilments to her
every wish.

In an empty sky
and during a night's full moon
It was then
A magnificence occured
The Moon smiled at her.

And in that very moment
She, had seen the light.
Somehow, hopeful,
She knew,
This ordeal she would survive.

Because the Moon spoke to Her.

Signed, Freedom
@wordsinaheartbeat

Shielded

Many emotions running through
I thought nothing would change my love for you
The beats in my heart remained strong and true
Until you branded me a fool.

But feelings of hate will never reach my flesh and bones
I am shielded no matter what you do
No act of yours could ever break me,
Or my soul, in two.

That's what it means to love unconditionally
To be armoured with so much purity
That even after everything
I am still able to love,

Effortlessly.

Signed, Freedom
@wordsinaheartbeat

A Queen is Rising

What you see
Underneath the pain and hurt
I'm still the same me.
You didn't make me bitter, no
You helped me find a new strength in me.
Your lies and disrespect
Look at me now, a wiser me.
A new appreciation for all that I am,
I learnt to love more of me.
Not dwelling no more on what could have been.
I learnt from the experiences,
And all the lessons you taught me
And I'm thankful to you
For awakening the fire in me.

A Queen is rising.

Signed, Freedom
@wordsinaheartbeat

I Loved You

I loved you.
I loved you until I could no longer.
With all my heart I loved you
Until loving you became unbearable.
You made it impossible to love.
With every kiss, every hug
With every ounce in me left
I gave it all to you.

Only to find out you never wanted my love.

Signed, Freedom
@wordsinaheartbeat

Blessings in Disguise

A sinister smile
And devious lies
Like the colours of rainbow
Not at one with himself
He prettied it all up
Wearing many faces
Teaching me some hard learned lessons
All part of the journey
And blessings in disguise.

Signed, Freedom
@wordsinaheartbeat

Epitome of Love

He was the villain in his own movie.
She was his featured movie star.
His eyes told the story
But his actions spoke much more.

She was the epitome of love
She didn't deserve this.
Such a sad and tragic ending.
And for this to be her first encounter
Of the real world.

Signed, Freedom
@wordsinaheartbeat

Living Without You

You taught me how to live
You taught me how to survive
You taught me how to carry on
How to endure emotional suffering and pain
You taught me many things,

All the things that meant living without you.

But now,
I am grateful for your lessons
As I enter a new world of hope
I finally see.
How I was your victim
Who's mind you had imprisoned
And I realise
That your fuck-ups were my golden ticket
To finally exit.

Signed, Freedom
@wordsinaheartbeat

You Killed Me

To have loved you
Was like dying
You killed me
Every single,
Time.

Signed, Freedom
@wordsinaheartbeat

Blind to See

I was never enough.
No matter what I did
You never really wanted me.

How was I so blind to see?

To think that you were mine
When all this time
You were creeping around.
Lying.
Whilst I,
Was at home alone,
Crying.

But you see,
I wasn't the blind one.
It was you,
Who was blinded
In all your misery.

Signed, Freedom
@wordsinaheartbeat

Never there

Let that settle in, for a moment
Your selfishness was your flaw.
You didn't focus enough on her.
You made her suffer
And instinctively she always knew
You were another woman's lover.

For nearly a decade she was yours
And you treated her like a toy.
Leaving her heart numb
and body sore.

You were really never sober; Never there;
In body, present, maybe.
But your mind was elsewhere.

Signed, Freedom
@wordsinaheartbeat

Once More

Make me feel wild.
For I longed to be loved
By you.

Drowned in emotion
My heart numbed, floating ashore.

Lost, yet wanting to feel the love
I never really felt,
Once more.

Signed, Freedom
@wordsinaheartbeat

Under Your Spell

Unbeknown to you
I was under your spell.
I longed for your lips, your eyes
And you kissing my neck
The best feeling
I ever felt.

I was in love with you
More than you ever knew.
Your body and soul
I couldn't set apart the two.
That's where I went wrong.
Because, I ended up the fool.

Clearly I misunderstood
Thinking the love we shared
Was somehow different
Unlike the rest, loyal and true.
But I was mistaken to think
That you loved me like I did you.

Signed, Freedom
@wordsinaheartbeat

Far beyond your reach

Let your poison reach my veins, my heart has become accustomed to your toxic fumes.
Left breathless by your silence, when I'd question the way you'd make me feel.
'Paranoid' you'd get in a one word sentence in between.
But I only saw the good in you without anticipating that you'd strike again.
No feelings, just darkness in you. What I done to deserve any of this?
My response was always in raging anger, followed by river tears.
I cried and cared.
Punishing me, you always remained so silent and still.
Whilst I poured my heart out, you'd be thinking of your next lies that I might believe.
You broke me.
And I just couldn't understand why, because I knew my worth.
I tried but I was never enough, no matter what I did.
All I ever wanted was to feel your love, the way I needed to be loved.

But you were too busy catching fallen birds, whilst I
was always far beyond your reach.
But now I understand.

Signed, Freedom
@wordsinaheartbeat

A Symbolic Idol

Overwhelmed, yet she remained grateful,
For the happy times and times of despair.

From all the heartache she endured,
She learnt that to love, meant to love herself fully first.

She learnt to let her heartbeat with excitement
And to live like no one was watching.

Embodying every emotion
She was art expressed in all of her words and actions.
To those who knew her; exemplary,
She was a Symbolic Idol.

Signed, Freedom
@wordsinaheartbeat

A Genuine Love

She was a genuine girl who longed for a genuine love.
Wanting to be appreciated for all that she was;
That is, the good, and any bad.
To be kissed with so much passion,
A real kind of love.
One that would move mountains
Just to see her eyes light up and smile.
And she wouldn't settle for anything less.
She had faith that she would find it in this world or the next,
Somehow.

Signed, Freedom
@wordsinaheartbeat

So Numb

What's in front of her
She cannot see.
So numb she cannot feel.
Walking blindly into the unknown
Planting her thoughts as seeds of purpose.
Leaving behind a trail.
So if she ever gets lost on her journey,
She can find her way, back again.

Signed, Freedom
@wordsinaheartbeat

She Forgave Her Past

Free at Last
Looking to the future
She forgave her past.

The last few years had been a whirlwind
Of good and bad
But more like a bad dream.
Like she overdosed
A half-conscious state
Stuck in a trance.

But finally she rose up.
Spreading her wings
She was,
Free at last.

Signed, Freedom
@wordsinaheartbeat

The Last Time

She said goodbye to him, for the last time.

And for the first time, he understood.
This time she wasn't changing her mind.
It really was for good.

Signed, Freedom
@wordsinaheartbeat

Troubled Soul

Troubled soul,
Pretending to be happy
But it was all for show.

Pretty soul,
Pretending to be strong
Draining herself for far too long.

Holding back her tears,
Silently drowning, in her own fears.

But still she felt safer in her dark place.
Her pretend, happy place.

Distancing herself, so she didn't have to explain.
She was a lone wolf.
She couldn't be saved.

Signed, Freedom
@wordsinaheartbeat

Goddess of the Sun

She was in a world of her own,
Fighting battles all alone.

A soul so old
Older than her body
Or her mind
She was her mind's eye.

A hidden gem
With unbreakable spirit;
Spreading love and light
Beyond.

A Goddess of the Sun.

Signed, Freedom
@wordsinaheartbeat

Unconditional Love

Lost at first sight;
Blinded by the brightness in his eyes

Lost in his sadness hidden behind every smile.

She was his angel of rescue
Washing the tears away with every tide.
Giving him unconditional love,
For the sadness that he kept hidden in his heart.

Signed, Freedom
**@*wordsinaheartbeat*

In the middle of the night

In the middle of the night;
She lay there,
Thinking.

Staring profoundly,
At her phone screen
In the dark.

Words in her head appearing.
Like little bright lights
Like she's dreaming.

But not, wide awake;
She lay there
Thinking.

How ambiguous
Life is.

Signed, Freedom
@wordsinaheartbeat

Insomnia

Anxiety,
Keeps her awake.
Anxiety,
Is endless worry;
Fear of what hasn't happened yet.
Anxiety,
She is her laughter and her pain.
Anxiety,
Is emotion, rushing through her veins.
Anxiety,
Like insomnia, is what keeps her awake.

Signed, Freedom
@wordsinaheartbeat

I Asked the Angels

I asked the Angels,
What's my purpose for being here?
Walking into the unknown,
So interconnected to the universe
Why is it that I do not fear?
And on this path to self-discovery;
I noticed more and more
The beauty and love that surrounds me.
And I thank the powers above;
For this gift, of Enlightening me.

Signed, Freedom
@wordsinaheartbeat

Silenced

Her feelings were frozen words
Silenced, at the tip of her tongue.

A numbness not many could bear
The heaviness in her heart
A pain that resided there.

Lost in a maze of her own thoughts;
Going round in circles
Searching for a part of her that was lost.

She was a solitary soul
Yet she wanted to be heard
So through her silence, finally,
She spoke.

Signed, Freedom
@wordsinaheartbeat

Mesmerised

Gazing, at a dark and perpetual sky,
Endless, like the emptiness
Inside of her;
And the teardrops she cried.

Mesmerised,
By the infinite possibilities of the night
She grew strong;
Amidst the dark,
Like a bright light
Turned on.

Signed, Freedom
@wordsinaheartbeat

She Couldn't Be Heard

Her words prompted nothing
It was useless
Her mind, clueless
Why She couldn't be heard.

Her fighting thoughts
Lost, amidst the eternal silence of the universe
Her heart static, as it silently bled.
Helpless, She gave up trying
To fight this curse.

Was her reason for being
To love this much
So it always hurts.

Signed, Freedom
@wordsinaheartbeat

Anxious

Feel the rhythm of her heart
Beating fast, palms are sweaty
So, anxious, two worlds apart.
Doesn't know where she's at.
Lost in transition from A to B.
With no rule book
Not how things were supposed to be.
But finally in a place where she can see.

Signed, Freedom
@wordsinaheartbeat

Fire in The Stars

She was a passionate lover
With beauty in her soul
A burning desire
Like fire in the stars.

Signed, Freedom
@wordsinaheartbeat

Unsettled Mind

A deep darkness in her heart,
Struck like thunder in the night.
A heavy cloudburst, a dark sky,
She had thunderstorms reflecting in her eyes.
Mirroring her soul,
And, unsettled mind.

Signed, Freedom
@wordsinaheartbeat

Love Her

See her, Feel her, Touch her, Kiss Her
Lover her truly.
Appreciate all of her.
Before it's too late.

Signed, Freedom
@wordsinaheartbeat

Lost for Words

Stuck between two contradicting worlds;
She didn't know
If it is for better or worse
To feel so much
The need for him or his love;
That sometimes
She found herself
Lost for Words.

Signed, Freedom
@wordsinaheartbeat

Poison

She was sweet.
But her words;
Her words were poison;
Spilling from her lips.

Signed, Freedom
@wordsinaheartbeat

Lover of Life

She shone bright,
Across the dark blued-sky.
She was like starlight,
A dreamy sight.
Wherever she went
She went with a smile.
It was her weapon,
Her weapon of love.
Spreading happiness
She was a lover of life.

Signed, Freedom
@wordsinaheartbeat

A Woman of Strength

He knows she is a woman of strength.
Like, he can feel the power in her veins.
And just by her presence,
He felt intimidated.
But this was never her intention.

Signed, Freedom
@wordsinaheartbeat

Sadness in Her Eyes

So much sadness in her eyes.
So much love in the same smile.
Both a blessing and a curse;
To feel everything so deeply,
Every bit of emotion,
To the core and in her bones.

Signed, Freedom
@wordsinaheartbeat

Head-Strong

She's head-strong.
Yet, he somehow plays with her mind.
With his perfect face
And beautiful eyes.
He gets to her,
A heartbeat at a time.

Signed, Freedom
@wordsinaheartbeat

Her Mind

Late at night,
She can't sleep.
Her Mind so busy,
Thought's won't leave.
Bewildered,
She lay still.
Late night
Musing;
Trapped in her thoughts
Whilst dozing off to sleep.

Signed, Freedom
***@wordsinaheartbeat*to*

Past Midnight

Hand to hand
Holding tight.
Body to body
Touching her right.
Lips to neck
A soft bite.
Skin to skin,
It's past midnight
He can't resist.
She's magnetite.

Signed, Freedom
@wordsinaheartbeat

A Spiritual Journey

My heart wonders,
Not knowing what for.
A fire burning in my soul.
Deep down into the subconscious,
Searching deep for more.
And still.
Not knowing what for.

Signed, Freedom
@wordsinaheartbeat

Love Myself

Love me or don't.
It truly doesn't make a difference
I've learnt to love myself.
And no better love ever existed.

Signed, Freedom
@wordsinaheartbeat

Solar Eclipse

Their heart coexisted in the subconscious sense.
She was the moon; Shadowing the sun.
Day turned into night; a solar-eclipse, occurred.
And just like that, for a few moments,
Two in their existence, became one.

Signed, Freedom
@wordsinaheartbeat

His Smile

On her rainy days,
His smile;
Was like the sun
Shining upon her.
He lit up her world
And didn't even know it.

Signed, Freedom
@wordsinaheartbeat

Lust

We don't always end up with those
who truly deserve us.
We end up ignoring the right ones.
Those who really crave for us.
Short-sighted and even blinded
by a momentary feeling
which we mistake for love.
We make sacrifices,
Only to find out that all this time
We have been at the mercy
Of a thing called, Lust.

Signed, Freedom
@wordsinaheartbeat

An Angel in Disguise

She was lost, now she's found.
Surrounded by so much darkness,
A bright light, so profound.
From the edge of the earth, looking down.
An angel in disguise, walking the ground.

Signed, Freedom
@wordsinaheartbeat

Incomplete

Searching from within,
For something old
Or rather something new.
Finding the missing clue.
She envisaged a bigger purpose.
What? Where?
She hadn't a clue.

Feeling incomplete
Looking for
When or where her heart
Felt most at peace.
She was fearless
In her pursuit.

Signed, Freedom
@wordsinaheartbeat

Art

She was like
Abstract Art.
She painted thoughts in your mind.
With no real depiction
Leaving you empty inside.
A raw and heavy feeling
Never fully explored.
A limitless composition
With endless possibilities.
A disposition.

Signed, Freedom
@wordsinaheartbeat

Daydream

Stuck in-between
Listening to her head, or
Leading with her heart
Which meant trusting her gut.
Feeling so lost, still caring so much.
With no one there to understand.
She lived in a daydream,
With every heartbeat
A Hypnotic trance.

Signed, Freedom
@wordsinaheartbeat

His Eyes

It's his eyes.
It's all in his eyes.
They get her every time.
Striking her down
Whilst purposefully gazing at her.
She, calm as the night.
His eyes, upon her darkness
A glaring light.

Signed, Freedom
@wordsinaheartbeat

Him

It was always about him.
But he was too side-tracked
And blind to see.

Signed, Freedom
@wordsinaheartbeat

He

Head had gotten inside her head.
Causing her so much grief
and so much pain.
Until he became a lesson learnt.

Signed, Freedom
@wordsinaheartbeat

In Love

In Love.
Two bodies floating in the air.
Synchronised.

Like the deep roots of a rose.
Intertwined.

Tied in their promise
Forever and always
To love and to hold.

In Love,
Words used so freely.
Loosing their true meaning.

Signed, Freedom
@wordsinaheartbeat

Feel

As the Sun
Rises each day
A powerful energy;
Selflessly reborn.
All the colours of the rainbow
Reflecting upon earth.
A vital force striking her
With Light, Love and Hope
Her heart awakened,
To feel again.

Signed, Freedom
@*wordsinaheartbeat*ateart

Good-Hearts

Like echoes of a thousand lost souls,
Screaming thoughts, inside her head.

Strong-minded and strong hearted.
She, unable to comprehend;

Why is it that the good-hearts,
Are the ones left damaged and hurt?

Signed, Freedom
@*wordsinaheartbeat*

Tamed

Broken and heart-restrained,
Even he, couldn't keep her sane.
An angel with broken wings
Far too wild to be tamed.
She had already seen hell,
Through all his lies
And twisted games.

Signed, Freedom
@wordsinaheartbeat

Divine

Light her up,
Strip her down.
Her body; his temple.
Godlike and Divine.

Signed, Freedom
@wordsinaheartbeat

Reddish Lips

Her Lips, tasted like venom.
Whilst biting onto his;
She was toxic
But tasted sweet.
Finally, succumbed to his temptation,
A euphoric sensation.
Leaning forward for more.
A hands-on taste
Of her reddish lips.

Signed, Freedom
@wordsinaheartbeat

Fire Burn

She had that effect on him.
Once she got close
Her touch
A hot flame
Like a Fire burn;
He yearned for her,
She was
Heaven on Earth.

Signed, Freedom
@wordsinaheartbeat

Lost Souls

Like Lost souls,
Searching in the dark.

With words left unsaid
Their worlds were drifting apart
His silence, leaving a tainted mark.

Like a lucid dream
Stuck in a dark place
Worlds apart.

Signed, Freedom
@*wordsinaheartbeat*

A Fairy-Tale

It was a bittersweet story,
With a fairy-tale ending
For her.

Signed, Freedom
@wordsinaheartbeat

Falling

She was the tree that stood still,
Rooted to the solid ground.
So sure of herself,
Until he came into her life.

All of a sudden this feeling, She, didn't recognise.
Her heart felt unsettled,
Like the autumn leaves,
A soft and rustling sound.

And all of a sudden,
Heart-felt rushing excitement.
She was head over heels,
And love-bound.

Falling softly like the leaves,
But never touching the ground.
Her head in the clouds
A real kind of love,
She thought she had found.

Signed, Freedom
@wordsinaheartbeat

A Rose with Thorns

She was
A single rose with thorns that pricked.

Only he
Who valued her worth could hold her.

She was
Not for the faint-hearted or weak.

Signed, Freedom
@wordsinaheartbeat

Destiny

It was destiny.
She was certain,
They were meant to be.

She was his craving'
And for her, always
That little bit more of him.

Signed, Freedom
@wordsinaheartbeat

Piercing-Eyes

Got her feeling at the first sight of you.
Your aura, so bright and colourful.
Your skin, soft-white,
And those piercing green eyes.
You smiled at her
Like the moon.

Signed, Freedom
@wordsinaheartbeat

Words in a Heartbeat

When my thoughts would turn to you,
Words in a Heartbeat
Came rushing through;
A story about twin souls
In love
Or so I thought of
As being us.

Signed, Freedom
@wordsinaheartbeat

Dying Love,

Empty
On the inside
With so much love to give
But nothing more
Left for him.

A dying love
Long overdue
She walked away
As he stood still.

Signed, Freedom
@wordsinaheartbeat

The End

The End.
Staring at him
She said.

No more,
Heart-ache or Pain.

And just like that;
Her Sadness
Wind-blown
Vaporised into thin air.

Signed, Freedom
@wordsinaheartbeat

The Sun Rose

As the sun rose
She looked up and saw a reflection of the heavens,
In Him.

Signed, Freedom
@wordsinaheartbeat

The Galaxy

A place where millions and billions of stars resided,
Optimally in their imperfect synergy, aligned.

A mirror reflection of him and her combined.

Signed, Freedom
@wordsinaheartbeat

Motionless

Laying there, her body motionless
eyes staring at the white-painted ceiling.
Her mind wide-awake,
Contemplating and Over-thinking.
Her heart sinking,
Stuck between the future, present and
The beginning.

A motionless-feeling.

Signed, Freedom
@wordsinaheartbeat

She Was A Storm;

Her heart often drifted like a craft lost at Sea.
Keeping both oars in the water,
Her mood often changed like the atmosphere.

She was a storm;
Thunder, lightning,
And the rain lived within her.

Signed, Freedom
@wordsinaheartbeat

Shine my light.

Like the Moon,
Which circles the Sun.
I shine my light
No matter where I am.

Signed, Freedom
@wordsinaheartbeat

Nights Sky;

Up, upon the dark nights ceiling,
A tiny star above was beaming.

Shooting across the nights sky,
A beautiful star was burning out.
Preparing
To say Goodbye.

Signed, Freedom
@wordsinaheartbeat

Fearless Heart,

When in pressure,
From the fears of failure…
Try to take a leap of faith
Should your ghosted thoughts haunt you again.

Thoughts, that your heart conjured,
A lost feeling that only your heart endured.

Living in this state of depression,
Speak up and let it be known
I promise,
You are not alone.

Signed, Freedom
@wordsinaheartbeat

Strength Is A Virtue

Strength is a virtue within us all.
But at times we too can fall.
So Deep, Heavy-hearted,
Like an anchor pulling on our hearts-strings.

The heart can bear so much emotion;
Such a powerful and meaningful notion,
To simultaneously feel a little of everything;
Happiness, Love and Suffering.

But like the Bee that finds a flower,
It's about getting 'loves dose' from one another.
Such an emotional sting,
Which blossomed from a one time fling'
To him buying her, that diamond ring.

The constant feeling of confusion and being
misunderstood;
Now she knows she was young and acted too soon.

Years ahead,
She finally accepted this as her fate
Whilst soul searching for her Passion and Truth.

Showing more love,
And doing God's good.

Signed, Freedom
@wordsinaheartbeat

With the Heart,

With the Heart she did write –
With the Mind she did speak,
About how she felt so insecure and weak,
A darkened tear, reflecting the nights sky,
Would slowly fall upon her cheek.

Her heart felt so clouded,
Overcrowded; with the confused thoughts,
That stormed inside her head.

And yet, the painful feelings slowly began to burn,
Out of existence; but her memories still remained.

Signed, Freedom
@wordsinaheartbeat

What the Heart felt,

What the Heart felt, she needed it to be heard.
For a long time, she had so very-deeply cared,
Like a brittle needle, hanging loose on a thread,
She wondered why; her poor heart had been so sadly misled.

Giving herself to him, her entire soul and energy
Like the ocean feeds the earth, giving so selflessly.

She was like water, kind and fierce.
A heart that flowed freely,
Whilst her soul; had waves crashing within.

HE, was like the views upon earth;
Soft grounds' were his lies
Piercing greenery were his eyes
No emotion or remorse
Like the earth's core, hard as iron inside.

Signed, Freedom
@wordsinaheartbeat

The Untold Love Story,

Love is when Two hearts meet at parallel,
Slowly Learning how to love in heaven and in hell.

Unconditionally falling for each other, so fast
Their souls feel, like life-time lovers, they will last.

But even with their hearts intertwined and so perfectly aligned.
Their love was very much left, in many ways undefined.

Signed, Freedom
@wordsinaheartbeat

Words from the Heart

Words from the heart…on what is Pain?
An ever-lasting, emotional stain?

Heart skips a beat, got me feeling' light and faint.

These river teas of mine, start strolling down; as if I'm crying but in the rain.
What is pain, but a heart-felt strain, expect sunshine yet 'hit by thunder' goes the saying!

When my hearts' beating, my soul starts speaking, I feel myself weakening upon each tear dripping

…and with the second heartbeat, two beats gone, I ask myself 'where did I go wrong'!

A few seconds can take so long, but the third beat becomes my song, and

Pain is the feeling that has made me so strong.

Signed, Freedom
@wordsinaheartbeat

Together as one

She could see gazing across an endless sky
Stars amidst the dark shining their light
A feeling came over her, feeling so mesmerised.

She could see love in its simplest form
One star helping another shine
…and stars falling, but not before their time.

She could see a light so profound upon
The earth and its' heavenly skies
Two realms of existence coming together as one.
That was what she wanted love to feel like.

Signed, Freedom
@wordsinaheartbeat